WHERE THE LOST THINGS GO

WHERE THE LOST THINGS GO

A Lent course based on
Mary Poppins Returns

LUCY BERRY

DARTON · LONGMAN + TODD

First published in 2019 by
Darton, Longman and Todd Ltd
1 Spencer Court
140 – 142 Wandsworth High Street
London SW18 4JJ

ISBN 978-0-232-53440-5

A catalogue record for this book is available from the British Library

Bible quotations taken from The Revised New Jerusalem Bible,
published and copyright © 2019 by Darton, Longman and Todd and
Penguin Random House

Designed and produced by Judy Linard
Printed and bound Ashford Colour Press, Gosport

AN EARLY NOTE!

I naturally mention Mary Poppins many, many times in this book! To make life easier, please note that where I refer to Mary Poppins the character, her name appears in roman type, whereas when I refer to the books or the films, you will see them written in italics: *Mary Poppins*/ *Mary Poppins Returns*.

All Bible quotations are taken from the *Revised New Jerusalem Bible*.

CONTENTS

INTRODUCTION

Stories we tell

The scientists tell us that, ultimately, what separates humans
from animals is that we tell stories. We tell each other
stories all the time. And from all the large and small stories
we hear, throughout our lives, we extract information.
But we also extract meaning! We hear people recounting
their stories on buses and trains, on the radio and TV, on
the internet and on social media. They can be tiny little
everyday stories about getting wet in the rain… or huge
ones about bombs or birth. But they are always told by
someone who *felt* them. Bible stories are no different; they
are told to us, down the centuries, by people who *felt* them.
And all the stories that humans tell each other follow the
same pattern: an event, followed by its meaning.

The obvious story

Two questions need to be asked about any story. The first
one is: 'What happened?'

Let's look at a simple story about getting caught in
the rain, which you might hear anywhere …

*'I was at this freezing-cold, stupid bus-stop, in the
middle of nowhere. And then – oh my gosh – so*

*maddening – it bucketed down ... no umbrella ...
no jacket ... the sky just opened! (I mean I'm not as
young as I was.) And when I finally got to my son's
place I had to change into one of his tracksuits until
my clothes dried out!'*

The events of that story are obvious: the teller got soaked
on a cold day, far from shelter.

That is the 'actual' part of the story.

What the story means underneath

The second question we need to ask is: What is the story
about?

So, what *is* this rain-story telling us, apart from facts?
What is the meaning? Well ... that's not nearly so obvious
and it is definitely open for discussion. But if we look for
the feeling that prompted the telling of this tiny story, we
are very likely to find a meaning – or two, or three. So,
is the teller talking about undergoing mild discomfort, or
an ordeal? Was the event irritating or alarming? Is there
vulnerability in the story, or merely frustration? Is there
resignation to the onset of old age? Or celebration of the
sanctuary of a good parent-child relationship? To know
what any story is 'about' takes digging and interpretation.

Bible stories

The Bible was written across many, many centuries by
people who felt things strongly. The writer of each story
wants you to know what he's *feeling*. (Yes, it was most
probably a 'he'.) And those stories are told in order to

convey the meaning of specific events. But story-tellers, even the narrators of Bible stories, are only partly in control of their stories. That is true of every story ever told. The hearer – that's you – also decides …

Jesus understood this very well. He knew that whatever story you tell, each listener will decide, for better or worse, what that story means. The way he told his parables is a case in point. Mark's handful of sentences about a handful of seeds is a story of momentous meaning. The event in the parable is the sowing and the growing. That's the 'actual' bit. But what's it about? What did Jesus *feel* so deeply that he needed to tell us? What is it about that seed-story that grows within us still? Jesus says that, if we have 'ears to hear' we will discover a meaning. And he trusts us to discover it.

God in the story

I approach *every* story believing that God is present in it; whether the story-teller intends it or not. Philip Pullman, the author of the children's *His Dark Materials* trilogy cannot believe in God. Those three beautiful books are an attempted rebuttal of the God's existence. In an interview with *The New Yorker* on 26 December 2005, Pullman stated: *'I don't profess any religion; I don't think it's possible that there is a God; I have the greatest difficulty in understanding what is meant by the words 'spiritual' or 'spirituality'.*

What Mr Pullman believes or doubts can't be proved or disproved. But, ironically, his attempt to deny God brings the possibility of a deity centrally into his stories. To be told 'Do not think about an elephant!' is a brisk way to get us thinking of an elephant. To claim 'God does not exist' brings me, at least, closer to my God and my faith.

Mr Pullman's worldview is manifested in his books. He shows us a world where religion, at its worst, is present, and where God seems absent or non-existent. But his justified mistrust of organised religion has prompted many of us to think more carefully about the differences between faith and 'True Faiths'. In stories where horror and injustice are overcome by loyalty, perseverance and sacrifice, can we say that God is *not* depicted?

God is present in every story. Not usually as a character, not always with agency, but always there… In our little rain-story, we can see God in the rain, and in the love of the parent-child relationship. In a bomb-story we see Christ, crucified, among those wounded in the explosion; and we see The Spirit, impelling loving souls forward into acts of risk and salvation. In a birth-story, God is in the utter mystery of the mingling of biology, humanity and divinity.

Skating or digging

With any book, any film, any human story, any Bible story, we have a choice: we can skate on the surface observing events … or we can dig for meaning. Even with Hollywood stories (predominantly crafted to entertain and to make money), there's a lot more than mere commerce going on. God may not be written in, but God is always present.

Mary Poppins Returns seems, on the surface, merely to be whimsy. You can watch it at that level. But there are substantial themes running through the film. Most, though not all, are intentional. As we move through this course, we can watch the great *Disney* fun-factory as it tries to deal lightly with massive themes of love, money, death, hope, home, displacement, loss, good and evil. It will be up to you to decide what point the film is making, or trying to make. What is the film really about? Where is God present in the film? What significance can we safely attach to a film which seems at first viewing to be a fairy-story? Where is the meaning for *us*?

Many whispering voices

In every story there has to be a voice. If you hear a story from a friend, or someone on the bus, it is easy to know *whose* story it is. But in written stories, especially older stories, there are voices that it's easy to miss. They are the whispering voices of the people who created, or wrote down, the story: the Narrators.

In the Bible, our narrators are the psalmists, the poets, the lawyers, the historians, the gospel writers, all aching for our attention. They care that you listen! In the same way that you or I try to find the *exact* words to express ourselves, so do these people. In the same way that we use words to carry a point, so do they. Of course, I'm talking in the present tense, because words, however ancient or modern, happen to us in the *now* – and can influence us *now*. Remember that stories don't tell themselves. When a story 'speaks' to us, we must be aware that a narrator is having a say.

Some people say that all History should really be called 'his story'. That is because, even now, History is being chronicled mainly by men who see things (fairly understandably) from a male perspective. Across the millennia, the people who recounted most fictional and 'factual' stories have been men. The Bible is the same: the communities from which the books of the Bible come did not encourage female literacy.

Perhaps a *really* balanced account of an event, would, theoretically, be 'his-and-her-story'. But that's not how stories work! A story starts off from the mind and heart of one individual who needs to tell it. As soon as it is re-told, it alters. With each re-telling, it alters further; each voice adding and subtracting something from the original.

Here's a personal example: My father used to tell a sweet and funny story. It was Guy Fawkes night. Dad was seven. Dad's dad wouldn't let the family have their fireworks until after supper. But my dad couldn't wait. He finished his supper, pretended he was going upstairs, but went to gaze at the big bag of fireworks in the front room. He lit one firework at the open fire, without understanding how silly that was…and then he heard his father coming! So he stuffed the lighted firework back in the bag, and went back and sat down with the family … and ten minutes later: BOOM! BOOM! BOOM! ***BOOM!***

I cannot possibly tell you this story in the hilarious, lengthy way that my father told it. He told it from his own 'culprit' perspective, with plenty of his own characteristic swearing, and he told it nostalgically, about a family long dispersed. When he told it to my young son he missed out (most of) the swearing. My uncle, aged eight at the time of that explosive event, always used to tell the story very differently. There are bits of the story I have missed out, because they're not relevant here. If my son one day tells it to a child of his own, it will have altered more, with a different nostalgia for a beloved, foul-mouthed grandpa. One tiny family story, morphing in each generation.

ભ

The original creator and narrator of the *Mary Poppins* stories was Miss P. L. Travers. While they remained only in books, she had control of their telling. But once she had allowed them to be re-told by Disney, a host of voices, both creative and commercial, became involved in polishing, embellishing and altering them.

In truth, this isn't very different from the way the Bible has developed. There are two versions of the creation story in Genesis; the later one, written second, being the 'Adam's Rib' story. We cannot be sure what the intention of that second narrator was … but having two accounts changes how we think about each. There are *at least* three authors of the book of Isaiah. There are four Gospel writers, all emphasising points and excising material to get as close as possible to the truth as they see it. Three of them (Matthew, Mark and Luke) all draw on an even earlier narrative text which has been lost. So you see Disney is in good company: people like to re-tell a good story.

But Disney stories are commercial products. However charming they seem, they exist primarily for profit. As this course progresses it will be up to you to decide whether money, as motive and motif, has taken over the narrative of *Mary Poppins Returns*.

Disney will always serve up a happy ending. Light-hearted, optimistic 'dreams' are Disney's stock-in-trade. But Bible narrators have no share-holders and no stock-market considerations. Their goal is not money. There are fairly few simple happy endings in the Bible, nor were they mostly written to entertain (although they often do). Bible narrators do not want us to dream, except occasionally about the great Kingdom to come. They want to explore and interpret the meaning of life and death – and to discover where God and humankind fit together. They want to point us at their conclusions. They want us to change as a result. Their happy endings revolve around salvation, not solution. The wisest narrators leave us to ponder and wonder at God's interaction in the human world. Others, less wise and more anxious, try to tell us exactly what we should be thinking.

The voices of these human men echo down to us across millennia. They express ideas, opinions, hopes, yearnings, and they lay down the law. So, though we may be used to hearing *'This is the word of the Lord'*, we should beware. That particular wording was introduced into the new Anglican liturgies from the 1960s onwards. They were designated for scripture readings other than the Gospel. The phrase is a relatively new addition, embraced by some denominations.

It is important to consider so authoritative a statement; is everything in the Bible the word of God? Our Bible is a glorious, contradictory, happy and grief-stricken maelstrom of meaning. It offers us dollops of both divine truth and human agenda, mixed together sometimes in the same verse. To discern the word of God in the Bible, with the help of the Holy Spirit, is surely our task. So, it is our duty to question our narrators.

For example, narrators of the Bible did not question the existence of slavery, *whereas* we know it to be unnegotiably evil. The narrators could not conceive that women were as good as men, *whereas we* know they are. They believed that non-Jews were dirty, whereas we know that they are not. We eventually discerned these truths, not by ignoring our Bibles, but by reading them *more* deeply in the light of Jesus' life-death-Life story and with a focus on the Great Commandment.

Your own whispering voices

Have you ever had a conversation about the Bible inside your head? I have.

My 'exploring' voice (EV) asks a question which my 'orthodox' voice (OV) wants to squash. Here's an example:

EV: Why did Jesus curse the fig tree? What good did that do?

OV: He just did! You don't have to understand – just believe.

EV: But I don't quite believe it. It seems a bit unlike Jesus.

OV: Jesus can do what he likes, can't he?

EV: Ye … ess. But it's not loving or constructive. Maybe the narrator…

OV: Shut up about 'the narrator'. Jesus can do what he likes.

EV: Yes, he *can*. But maybe the narrator…

OV: Shut up about 'the narrator'. This is the word of **God**.

EV: Mm. And what about the Syrophoenician woman (Matthew 15:26). Why was Jesus rude to her?

OV: He wasn't really *rude*. He was joking.

EV: I don't think he was, you know.

OV: Shut *up*. He was.

Perhaps you have these inner arguments? Christians have been suffering with them for millennia. But don't let fear of your own ego, or fear of change, prevent you from humbly asking awkward questions. If people hadn't asked awkward questions about the Bible in the past, many and various white nations would still be kidnapping Africans in the belief that humans can 'own' humans. Don't *let* fear of unorthodoxy stop you from reading new things in old texts. Be wary of the risk-free voice which comes from within and which tries to squelch love and freedom for ourselves and others.

The Big Voice

The voice of God is, I suspect, too huge and too complex for us to hear, except in dark glimpses and 'in part' (1 Corinthians 13:8-12). Of *course* it is there, throughout the Bible, but speaking in such a variety of ways, through so many authors that we can't, with any humility, claim fully to comprehend it.

God is tough enough to let us question. And Jesus (our greatest clue to how and what God is), intentionally gave us parables to go away, to work out, to interpret for ourselves. In the light of this we may look through His lens of love, service, humour, acceptance and forgiveness at any part of the Bible, to try to discern its meaning.

During this course, as you read and discuss and meditate, don't be nudged by a narrator, another person, or by a nervous Orthodox Voice, into accepting an unexamined meaning. The most important voice is God's, and very mysterious. It is not in the whirlwind (1 Kings 19:11).

Approaching Easter with Disney?

You may be wondering how we can reconcile the dark lead-up to Easter with the dedicated cheeriness of Disney. Are we taking Lent sufficiently seriously, if we approach it through a Disney lens? After all, the events which bring us to Easter are utterly appalling. Every year we watch Christ pursue His lonely, unflinching campaign of Love, as evil elements within his own society (and among his own followers) betray, deny and kill him. It's not Disney.

Disney's intent, at all times, is to offer a spoonful of sugar; and the Bible's intent is never ever that. Healing to humankind, offered by the Easter story, can and must never go down 'in a delightful way'. Good Friday must be borne unsweetened, and Easter arrive un-gilded.

But the film promises much. It hints, even in the opening song, at hope and deliverance through faith. I believe we are here to explore whether it delivers that storyline. Walt Disney (whose ideals the Disney Corporation aim still to uphold) said two things which may, at least, reassure us of the film's intentions. He said:

I always like to look on the optimistic side of life, but I am realistic enough to know that life is a complex matter.

and:

We have created characters and animated them in the dimension of depth, revealing through them, to our perturbed world, that the things we have in common far outnumber and outweigh those that divide us.

Mary Poppins Returns is a far more complex film than first appears; and hugely more complex than the original *Mary Poppins* film. It does indeed portray a perturbed world. It will be up to you to decide whether the film says precisely what was intended. But dig here and you will not be disappointed. I hope your excavations give you a rich, meaningful way towards Easter – and the joy and the work beyond.

GETTING THE MOST FROM THIS COURSE

This book can be used by groups for discussion and study, or by individuals for personal devotion and reflection. Either way, you may want to begin each weekly session with a spontaneous prayer, and then conclude with the prayer provided for that particular week. Everyone's ideas, about the film and about their faith, will be different. Everyone's sincere approach will be shaped by life-experience. Each person's perspective is worth hearing. Each considered response is worth sharing with others and with God.

The structure and order of each of your five weekly sessions will always be the same. Whether you read this book alone or in company with a group and a group-leader, we ask that you:

- Pray a heart-felt and spontaneous prayer for the session ahead
- Watch specified clips from the film
- Notice how you *feel* about what you are seeing and hearing
- Consider what parts of your own life come to mind
- Consider each suggested Bible reading

- Explore how the Bible passages add to your understanding of the film – and vice versa
- Consider the questions supplied with each Bible passage
- Reflect on the ideas you most deeply understand. What personal experience brings you this understanding?
- Notice the ideas with which you don't easily connect. How might you grasp them better?
- If you wish, consider 'Other Questions' in the Leader's Section of this book
- If you wish, explore the songs in the 'A Funny Mixture' section at the end of this book.
- If it feels right, meditate and pray according to suggestions for each session.

Does any of this sound like a test? No, it's not a test! There are no wrong or right answers to the questions in this book. This is just a structured way of exploring the themes of the film in relation to aspects of faith.

The still small voice in personal reflection

If you notice an uncomfortable thought or feeling, don't push it away; God can bear whatever you're thinking, and God will give you the strength to recall tough things and think through hard questions. Remember: *Come to me, all ye are who are heavy laden, and I will give you rest.* The Lent journey is one which we take, through trouble, towards peace. Fear not.

The still small voice in the group

God is present in every group, but not always obvious. The still, small voice of God can come unexpectedly, often from a disregarded person. It can't be heard when we're not listening faithfully. Where kindness and safety are operating it's audible. It's more important that God speaks than that we do. So, if you are studying this as part of a group:

- **Confidentiality** is safety. It allows people to talk authentically and openly without fear of gossip. At the start of each session, promise each other your confidentiality.
- **Interrupting** is unsafe. It suggests the speaker isn't worth listening to. It stops shy people from talking.
- **Sharing your own relevant experience** is generous. It gives breadth and reality to conversations, whereas theoretical discussions often lose a sense of the Spirit.
- **Contradicting** is unsafe. Even if one has no respect for what someone is saying, one can still respect their right to say it. Disagreeing gently (!) can open up good discussion.
- **Listening carefully** is kind. It recognises the worth of others.
- **Allowing some rambling** is kind. Not everyone thinks straight, or to the point. But everyone has the right to express themselves. Find gentle ways to move on from a ramble.
- **Inviting someone's opinion** is kind. Some people simply cannot 'bring themselves in' to a group conversation; and yet they may have great wisdom to offer.

SESSION 1

Were we dreaming?
Belief and unbelief

PRAYER

FILM CLIPS

Clip 1:   00.00 – 00.30 The *Disney* ident
Clip 2:   23.00 – 26.00 Mary's return to 17 Cherry Tree
          Lane
Clip 3:   1.55.16 – 1.57.50 Michael remembers

FOR YOU TO THINK ABOUT

> ***Don't believe the things you've read!***
> ***You never know what's up ahead …***

As Jack cycles through the streets of London, putting
out the lights, he is introducing us to a promise. He is
reassuring us, even before the action has begun, that we
will see a happy ending. He is asking us to trust. So, we
watch the film on the basis that there may be trouble
ahead, but that everything will work out beautifully.

We can (if we're not careful), approach the Easter
story the same way: we know the ending will be all right,
so we may tell ourselves the middle doesn't matter. Or
maybe the middle is just too awful to think about. Or
too difficult to believe. Belief is a theme which runs,

strangely, at the heart of this story. The Banks family need a miracle.

As Mary Poppins touches down, the little world of the Banks family, and the larger global picture are both in a sad state. Michael Banks, grown to adulthood now (though not perhaps very grown-up), is in emotional and financial turmoil. Britain is in the midst of the Great Depression. There could not be a better time for Mary Poppins to appear. But to her old charges, Jane and Michael, she seems merely a figure from the past. They no longer believe in her magic.

It is interesting to see how differently the people of 17 Cherry Tree Lane respond to Mary Poppins. The three young children soon believe she can do anything. Michael is initially too hopeless to have faith in her; he has money on his mind and has reduced her to an expense. Jane, too, has ceased to believe; she is taken up with social issues (as her mother before her) and recognises Mary Poppins' principal worth only as an organising force in a chaotic household. Ellen, the pragmatist, greets her as if she has never been away. As the film progresses, it is the person in the greatest distress whose beliefs will change the most. As outside observers of a disintegrating domestic situation, we can see that Mary Poppins' return, and her ruthlessly positive attitude, herald a change for the better. The narrative is setting Mary Poppins up as saviour. However, it won't be Mary Poppins who saves the day.

It is possible to look at the different characters as different approaches to faith. Georgie, the youngest child is joyfully open to everything. The twins, John and Annabel, have come to trust, above all else, in the efficacy of their own actions. They are practical, and vocal in their self-sufficiency. Michael, in his despair cannot focus on hope; he digs in dusty places for guarantees. Jane, a person of resolute cheerfulness, enjoys her childhood memories sentimentally, without believing in their accuracy. Ellen takes for granted an unbroken relationship; she takes up where she left off. The devoted believer, the lamplighter and 'keeper of the flame', does not live in the house.

Of course, none of us are just one thing. Depending on our predicaments and fortunes, our support and our background, we move between different kinds and intensities of faith during our lives. The jolliness which a person exhibits may be their only coping strategy. Self-sufficiency may obscure the lonely terror that no-one can help. The cover is, truly, 'not the book'. Which Banks family-member reflects your own approach to faith? Or are you more like Jack, the prophet of the piece, whose faith is unaltering and whose trust is firm?

'Soon the Slump will disappear. It won't be long …'

Depression is a word that Disney chooses to avoid, even though it is the recognised name for what both Michael and his era are undergoing. 'Slump' is their cheerier replacement. But depression, of a soul or a society, is a ghastly business. It happens gradually and invisibly and takes courage and time to confront and to dispel. Michael has made a mess of his personal finances and so has the Britain of the 1930s.

This film, unlike the original *Mary Poppins* is intentionally set in very troubled times. In October 1932, at the conclusion of an exhausting month-long 'hunger march' from the North of England to London, violence broke out between police and protestors in Hyde Park: 75 civilians were listed as injured. Oswald Mosley established the British Union of Fascists in the same year, and was responsible for whipping up organised hatred against Jews; the 'Battle of Cable Street' in London's East End being a horrifying example. Disney is recalling a time when sections of society blamed other classes, cultures and faiths for national trouble. We see something similar happening in places far and near today.

But this is a *Mary Poppins* film! It has turned a depression squarely into a 'slump'. Hunger is only hinted at as Jack casually throws an apple to a man queuing for food. Financial collapse is signified by the mounting number of house-repossessions which the lawyers Gooding and Frye are executing for the bank.

No direct connections are made between Michael's woes and Britain's hardship; but the two predicaments do echo one another. We might wonder why Disney set the film in a time of vast Western anxiety. Or we might assume that there is a quiet parallel being intentionally or inadvertently offered between those uncertain times and our own. No doubt we all wish, at times, for a personal-and-global Mary Poppins to solve our 'slumps'. Something is being said here, however quietly, about how unnegotiable life can be.

As Mary Poppins slides, incredibly, up the stairs into the nursery regions of Number 17 Cherry Tree Lane we know she will attend to *all* the Banks Children; not merely the three youngest. In her inflexible brightness, we expect she will change their lives and their fortunes. As the film nears its close (especially as the whole community dangle comfortably from balloons), Michael is no longer depressed.

Teasing out what Mary Poppins has actually achieved during the course of the story is difficult. Her relationship to reality is ultimately an odd one. She may sing an encouraging song. She may float through the sky. She may put back the clock. She may (secretly) care. But what has she done?

- What does it mean to say you believe 'in' something?
- Is there a difference between magic and miracle?

ↄ

FIRST BIBLE READING
John 3:1-10

There was one of the Pharisees called Nicodemus, a leader of the Jews. He came to Jesus by night and said, 'Rabbi, we know that you have come from God as a teacher; for no one could perform the signs that you do if God were not with him.' Jesus answered:

'Amen, Amen I say to you,
no one can see the kingdom of God
without being born from above.'

Nicodemus said, 'How can anyone be born who is already old? Can anyone enter into the mother's womb a second time and be born?' Jesus replied:

'Amen, Amen I say to you,
no one can enter the kingdom of God

without being born of water and the Spirit;
what is born of the flesh is flesh;
what is born of the Spirit is spirit.
Do not be surprised when I say:
You must be born from above.
The wind blows where it pleases.
You hear its sound,
but you do not know where it comes from
or where it goes.
So it is with everyone who is born of the Spirit.'

Nicodemus asked, 'How can that be?' Jesus replied, 'Are you the Teacher of Israel, and do not know these things!'

- Why is Nicodemus, the 'senior man', visiting Jesus?
- What is Jesus asking us to believe?
- Are the ways in which children see things silly?
- Why do you believe John felt he must tell us this story?

ও

SECOND BIBLE READING
1 Corinthians 13:9-12

For we know only in part and we prophesy only in part, but once perfection comes, the partial will be superfluous. When I was a child, I spoke as a child, I thought as a child, I reasoned as a child. When I became a man, I put aside the things of childhood, for now we see in a mirror, confusedly, but then we shall see face to face. Now I know only partially, then I shall know fully, just as I am fully known.

- What is Paul saying about our adult understanding of God?
- Is it compatible with what Jesus is saying to Nicodemus?
- What has maturity to do with faith and belief?
- Why do you believe Paul felt he must tell us this story?

ω

THIRD BIBLE READING
Mark 15:39

The centurion, who was standing opposite him, seeing that he had breathed his last, said, 'In truth this man was Son of God.'

- What does the centurion mean?
- What has made him believe in Jesus?
- Why do you believe Mark felt he must tell us this?

A Time for Further Discussion

Meditation – As we prepare for Easter:
Jesus of Nazareth, the grown man, referred to God as 'Abba' which means Daddy.

He believed in – and spoke about – the endlessly patient love of God for all God's children, faithful and disloyal. He delivered that love to us in miracles, in service, in stories and in selflessness.

Whatever our age, we are all God's children. Can we contemplate God as a Daddy? Let's try.

PRAYER
Daddy, you call us to believe in you. And we do!
But to believe in you is to subscribe to you,
and to subscribe to you is to serve you
and to serve you is to act for you:
to do your servant-work.

Daddy, you call us to believe in you. And we don't!
For to believe in you is to live for you,
to live with you, to live by you, and to live in you;
to trust in you, to be led by you,
into places we do not choose.

Daddy, take us back – or forward – to childlike trust.
Take our hand, our fears ...
our self-sufficiency, our doubt, our unbelief.
Take from us the huge temptation to 'know best'.
Save each of us from ourselves,
and gather us, your little children,
into your embrace.
Amen

If it suits you better, the prayer can be read back and forth between two halves of the group – like this:

PRAYER

Daddy, you call us to believe in you.
And we do!
But to believe in you is to subscribe to you,
and to subscribe to you is to serve you
and to serve you is to act for you:
to do your servant-work.

Daddy, you call us to believe in you.
And we don't!
For to believe in you is to live for you,
to live with you, to live by you, and to live in you;
to trust in you, to be led by you,
into places we do not choose.

Daddy, take us back – or forward – to childlike trust.
Take our hand, our fears...
our self-sufficiency, our doubt, our unbelief.
Take from us the huge temptation to 'know best'.
Save each of us from ourselves,
and gather us, your little children,
into your embrace.
Amen

SESSION 2

This can't be happening! Loss, denial and acceptance

PRAYER

FILM CLIPS
Clip 1:   15.48 – 18.18 'A Conversation'
Clip 2:   58.20 – 1.02.28 'The Place Where Lost Things Go'

FOR YOU TO THINK ABOUT

'I'm looking for the way things were.'

Everyone attached to the Banks household is mourning Kate, Michael's wife and the mother of his children. It is clear that she was both a loving and a practical person. From the little that we hear of her, she seems to have been the unspoken head of the family. In his grief, Michael has ceased to cope emotionally and practically. He has lost his bearings. The beloved backbone of his existence, the person on whom he relied to steer his family and his household, as well as their routines and their finances, has gone. We cannot guess at the man Michael was before Kate's death;

at present he seems only nominally an adult. He has taken a job which doesn't suit him and made huge, unilateral, disastrous financial decisions. His world is in free-fall.

Watching the original *Mary Poppins* film, it was difficult to feel sorry for Michael's father, who was depicted as pompous, silly, and out of touch. Michael's character is more loveable, similarly ineffectual, never comic. He is lost in a wilderness of pain, with no faith in anything except the departed Kate. Disney has moved far enough from cheeriness to give us, in Michael, one entirely authentic character.

Bereavement prompts feelings like no other loss and is governed by no timetable. It affects us physically and emotionally and our feelings of despair, anger and confusion arrive in great waves, and without warning. It is *the* most difficult kind of change we face, because to grieve is to confront a seemingly diminished future without one of the great pillars of our past. A year has passed since Kate's death. But anyone who has suffered a major bereavement knows that a year is no time at all to repair the shock of such a loss. Yet people seem to expect Michael to be himself again.

Michael's song, sung to his absent Kate, in the dusty loft of his mortgaged home, is one of yearning for the past and for lost things; a song to someone who cannot hear or help. His song springs from a place of tenderness and vulnerability. '*Where did you go?*', the last words of his song, probably resonate with us all. Michael is dealing – or not dealing – with the greatest mystery of all: where do the dead go?

ᘓ

We humans find acceptance difficult and denial easy. When someone dies, or when situations of great significance change, we are constantly '*looking for the way things were*'. We do it in every aspect and at every stage of life. We attempt to control the oncoming future. We try to ignore the pains of the present. We re-write the past to make it more comfortable. The truths of our lives are all around us and, as adults, we often try to avoid them. Young children are good at truth; presumably that is why Jesus loved them so.

The three Banks children have little support or empathy from their adults who are negotiating loss themselves in different ways. Ellen, who has known Michael all his life, carries on without referring to Kate's death. Her duties are getting harder and she expects Michael to sort them out. She shows little sympathy, but good humour; a traditional British way of coping, but not always a kind one. Jane is as unmotherly as her mother before her; wrapped up in wider social issues, she has barely noticed the deteriorating situation. The children are left to manage.

Actually, *all* change, bad or good, has loss attached to it. Even the best changes come at a cost. The move to a better home, for example, is almost always a move away from familiar routines, shops, neighbours. The arrival of a new baby is the end of many freedoms. The start of a new job, or the first days at a new school, come with nerve-wracking learning curves, new practices, new hierarchies. All change means letting go, and the changes we choose are difficult enough. The changes we do *not* choose, 'untimely' death especially, can call into question our old beliefs and can be painfully disorientating.

People in the Bible hated change too. The psalmist

aches to return, out of the strange land of Babylon. Jonah resents his call from God, and tries energetically to avoid it. Saul becomes violently paranoid at the popularity of David. The Pharisees send their Messiah to die, in vicious rejection of his ideas, his love and his popularity. The very men whose learning and calling could have assured him recognition and welcome are those who most powerfully deny him, and his Good News.

Denial can manifest in two ways: as flat refusal to accept a reality. Or as rejection of its gravity. But all denials, however pathetically understandable, simply do not work. Events continue to develop whether we deny them or not.

The greatest denial in the Bible, and the most human, is Peter's three-times denial of Christ. Peter has claimed Jesus as his Messiah, actually as *the* Messiah – and then pretends not to know him. The vastness of this can never be over-estimated. Peter is denying relationship with his God and with his best friend. And yet, what Peter does mirrors most of compromised, frightened humanity: he wants to save his own skin. Jesus, on the other hand, mirrors the divine: he accepts his peril as reality. True to his beliefs, he walks directly into the valley of the shadow, into open hatred and death.

How in heaven does the character of Mary Poppins fit into this? Well, surprisingly neatly it turns out. After all, part of Mary's DNA, in both films, is to take up a position of denial about things that undoubtedly happen. It is easy to see why, upon her return, Michael disbelieves and Jane doubts the magical events of the past.

Mary has never faced things head-on. Her song, *The Place Where Lost Things Go* is an attempt to comfort the three bereaved young children. It is a gentle, sweet song from a normally self-absorbed and starchy person, and it is full of understanding for the huge chasm of loss that the children face. But, even though the children find it a reassuring song, it is not altogether an honest one.

People often avoid discussing the finality of death with children. Perhaps we do it to protect them, perhaps to protect ourselves. Instead, many of us talk about being 'watched over', by our departed loved ones. Such a concept has no place in Christian or Judaic tradition. When Mary Poppins states that '*nothing's really left or lost without a trace*' she is confecting a very pretty denial: Kate is '*merely out of place*'.

In her own highly practical terms, Mary has characteristically reduced Michael's '*Where did you go*' question to something neat and manageable: Kate is in a celestial lost-property office, '*smiling from a star*'; a comfortable fairy-tale to contemplate, albeit dubious. Jesus, the glorious and challenging realist, never suggests that the dead watch over us. He weeps at the death of Lazarus and fears his own.

Like many of us, Mary is not confronting the reality of physical death. She has tidily consigned the mislaid Kate to exist alone in the stratosphere. She has offered the children no picture of resurrection, no Kingdom, no closeness with the Creator. The song is unsound, by any standard. While we, as Christians, believe in our Easter-reality of a killed-yet-living Lord, Disney offers something sugary and anodyne. Yet, even as Christians who offer hope and faith, we must avoid the dogma of faith-as-fact. There is no utter certainty. Mary has done what many of us do; denied that death is an ending. But for Christians that leaves us without Easter. There can be no resurrections for us without death. As the Banks children grow up, they must decide whether to continue to embrace Mary's sugary ideas, or to swallow crucifixion.

- Is Mary Poppins' approach sentimental, or spiritual?
- How do you deal with people who force you to confront your reality?
- Should we comfort children with things that can't be proved?

ϾϿ

FIRST BIBLE READING
Ecclesiastes 3:1-8

There is a season for everything, a time for every occupation under heaven:

a time to give birth and a time to die;
a time to plant and a time to uproot what has been planted;
a time to kill and a time to heal;
a time to knock down and a time to build up;
a time to weep and a time to laugh;
a time to mourn and a time to dance;
a time to throw stones away and a time to gather them in;
a time to embrace and a time to refrain from embracing;
a time to seek and a time to lose;
a time to keep and a time to discard;
a time to tear and a time to sew;
a time to keep silent and a time to speak;
a time to love and a time to hate;
a time for war and a time for peace.

- What makes this highly candid passage so comforting?
- What meaning do you attach to the line about stones?
- Is there loss in these lines?
- Why do you believe this poet felt he must tell us this?

ↄ

SECOND BIBLE READING
Mathew 22:23-29

That day some Sadducees approached him, denying that there is any resurrection, and they put this question to him, 'Teacher, Moses said, *If a man dies childless, his brother is to marry the widow, and raise children for his brother.* Now there were seven brothers among us; the first married and then died without children, leaving his wife to his brother; similarly also the second and third and so on to the seventh. Last of all the woman herself died. Now at the resurrection, whose wife among the seven will she be, since she had been married to them all?' Jesus answered them, 'You are wrong, because you understand neither the scriptures nor the power of God.'

- Why are the Sadducees asking this question?
- Why is Jesus so dismissive?
- Do you believe admission to heaven is governed by rules?

- Why do you believe Matthew felt he must tell us this story?

ↄ

THIRD BIBLE READING
Matthew 16:21-23

From then onwards Jesus began to show his disciples that he must go to Jerusalem and suffer grievously at the hands of the elders and chief priests and scribes and to be put to death and to be raised up on the third day. Then, taking him aside, Peter began to rebuke him, saying, 'Heaven preserve you, Lord, this must not happen to you.' But he turned and said to Peter, 'Get behind me, Satan! You are a stumbling-block to me, because you are thinking not as God thinks but as humans do.'

- Why is Peter unable to accept the truth?
- Why is Jesus so very angry with Peter?
- In what way is Peter a 'stumbling block'?
- Why do you believe Matthew felt he must tell us this story?

A Time for Further Discussion

Meditation – as we prepare for Easter
Jesus spoke about everything, including his torture and death, honestly. What is it in our past, present or future that we have not faced honestly? Are we brave enough to face it, with Jesus here beside us?

PRAYER

Lord,

You said the truth would set us free.

But we do not much like truth.

We do not like the pain and the muddle which you
watched and healed un-squeamishly.

If there is un-truth here, with us now,

help us notice it and mend it.

If there are things which we have not faced

or will not face, or cannot face,

lift our averted eyes to you and

make us brave in your service.

Amen

PRAYER

Lord,

You said the truth would set us free.

But we do not much like truth.

**We do not like the pain and the muddle which you
watched and healed un-squeamishly.**

If there is un-truth here, with us now,

help us notice it and mend it.

If there are things which we have not faced

or will not face, or cannot face,

lift our averted eyes to you and

make us brave in your service.

Amen

SESSION 3

The Banks children?
Or the bank's children?
Solution or salvation

PRAYER

FILM CLIPS
Clip 1:   53.15 – 57.45 Georgie's nightmare
Clip 2:   1.48.40 – 1.50.28 The real nightmare

FOR YOU TO THINK ABOUT

> *'And you'll achieve that sense of conquest*
> *as your affluence expands'*
>
> (Mary Poppins 1964)

P. L. Travers, author of the original *Mary Poppins* books did not name the Banks family randomly. 'Banks' was a meaningful word to her and an ambivalent one too. *Real* banks were highly significant in her early life. The Disney film, *Saving Mr Banks,* explores her childhood and the intense financial insecurity endured by her family, owing to the unreliability of her father, a charming and drunken bank-manager. It is a film well worth watching, for it explains the yearning which is written into every fibre of the *Mary Poppins* books: the yearning for a stable adult who can bring both joy and order to chaos.

The world into which Mary Poppins descends in this second film is much tougher than the one she left. London is hungry. Her first charges, Jane and Michael Banks have grown up, but not much. Michael has abandoned his artistic vocation to become a teller in the bank where his father used to work. He is heavily and perilously in debt; and he is employed by the very organisation which is out to destroy him. Anyone who takes out a mortgage has felt something between respect and fear for the power of their bank.

So the film may be offering a feel-good story, but money – the lack of it, the loss of it, and the need of it – drives the plot. Mass unemployment is only just visible, but it is there in the film. There is no food in the house when we first meet the Banks family, and within minutes they are also facing homelessness.

The Banks family's backstory is inextricably bound to the bank. Michael's remote and pompous and father, who we meet in the first *Mary Poppins* film, is hugely proud of his position working in the bank as his father did before him. In the course of the film and after many ups and downs, he is eventually made a director.

In spite of this, the theme of untrustworthy, dangerous bankers runs through both films. The ancient employers of the original Mr Banks are avaricious and very frightening.

(I remember feeling real alarm as a child, watching the young Michael being harassed for tuppence that he had saved to feed the birds.)

In our second film, William Weatherall Wilkins has become the villain of the piece: intent on repossessing the Banks' house. He is shown as callous, gloating and unprincipled. His pawns (one weak and foolish, one lovable) are the lawyers who Wilkins uses to carry out his repossessions. Wilkins has no redeeming features; he will be the only character *not* to be granted a heavenly balloon-ride at the close of the film.

After the global banking scandals of the last several decades, choosing a banker for a 'baddie' was probably an easy option for Disney. Lawyers, the other malefactors in the film, are currently also easy targets. But we need to ask ourselves the question: if bankers are bad, what about banks? And if banks are so bad, where do we – and Disney – stand on money? *Mary Poppins Returns* bankrolled Disney $150,000,000 in the US alone … Has Disney, with vast wealth and a phalanx of lawyers, examined its standpoint?

There is a strand of Christian thinking which yearns to do away entirely with the use of money, or – at the very least – with the charging of interest. This is very much in line with both traditional Islamic and Judaic religious thinking, which is against trapping poor people in debt. Indeed, how can we possibly 'make poverty history' while hungry families and hungry countries are in deepening debt to systems established solely to grow the wealth of the already wealthy?

There is another strand of thought, sometimes dignified with the name 'Prosperity Theology', which suggests that to love God, to work hard, and to have faith, will guarantee financial success. This is dangerous whimsy. If we regard financial success as God's reward, we must also assume the shadow-side argument: that poverty is God's punishment for not loving God enough, working hard enough, or having faith enough. To entertain such ideas promotes self-satisfaction and contempt amongst those who are coping, and despair amongst those who are struggling. Nor has it anything to do with the Good News. It confuses material solution with divine salvation.

Jesus never believed nor ever suggested that the acquisition of cash was a result of faith. In the wilderness we see him turning away from power, and therefore away from money. Through every gospel we see him travelling through the land as a peasant, walking from village to village on foot, with 'nowhere to lay his head' at night (Matthew 8:20). He moves amongst labourers, vineyard workers, tax collectors and prostitutes. He heals and preaches to the poorest, most downtrodden, most marginalised people; people who are never going to be a 'success'. He knows them to be the most fertile ground for seeds of salvation.

Jesus was clear about money. The parable about the poor man at Lazarus' gate is frightening in its clarity: rich people who do not help poor people are doomed (Luke 16:19-31). Christ's ministry boiled over (still does!) with indignation about inequity and the abuse of power. His temptations in the wilderness revolve around food, power and influence.

But the subject of wealth has been all too tempting for Disney: the power of money, as *the* saving force, has infused the film. The original *Mary Poppins* film ended with Mr Banks using Michael's tuppence to make a kite and to sail it joyfully with his often-neglected children. He has learned a lesson and turned over a new leaf. The moral of the story being that love wins over money. No such belief operates in the second film. In fact, the first film's narrative has been subverted to serve the second. The old story has been re-written: Michael's tuppence seems, after all, to have been invested! It has been sitting in the bank, all these years, accruing sufficient interest to pay off Michael's debt!

I do not believe that Disney realises precisely what it has done. But truth will out. Let us look for a moment at this amended story-arc that Disney has finally created; for I believe that God is showing us (if we have eyes to see and ears to hear), the unconscious narrative of Mammon:

A little boy saves up tuppence. He wants to visit the Bird Woman, an old lady who makes her living on the steps of St Paul's Cathedral by selling bird-seed for hungry pigeons. He has heard from his nanny that, 'All around the cathedral the saints and apostles look down as she sells her wares. Although you can't see it, you know they are smiling, when somebody shows that he cares...' But his father does not allow him to give the Bird Woman any money. She and her birds go without. His tuppence is invested instead. Many years down the line, his house is saved because his money did not go to the poor and the hungry.

I'm sure Disney would not own this as their position, but it is the story they tell: a lovely example of a narrator losing control of a narrative.

So, the Banks family problem is both created and solved by the bank. But what are we to make of this brace of films where anxiety about finance moves so near to the surface?

Perhaps you will want to consider these questions...

- Is life harder now than in 1964 when the original *Mary Poppins* was released?
- Is anything more powerful than money?
- Is it evil to charge interest?

૭

FIRST BIBLE READING
Isaiah 28:16

So the Lord GOD says this,
'See, I am laying a stone in Zion,
a granite stone, a precious cornerstone, set firm.
One who relies on this will not panic.'

- Many Bible passages are about building and buildings. Why?
- What is being promised in this verse?
- Is God all you need?
- Why do you believe Isaiah felt he must tell us this story?

૭

SECOND BIBLE READING
Luke 4:1–13

Filled with the Holy Spirit, Jesus left the Jordan and was led by the Spirit into the desert, for forty days being put to the test by the devil. During that time he ate nothing at all and when they were over he was hungry. Then the devil said to him,

'If you are Son of God, tell this stone to become a loaf.' But Jesus replied to him, 'Scripture says:

A human does not live on bread alone.'

Then, leading him to a height, the devil showed him in a moment of time all the kingdoms of the world and said to him, 'I will give you all this power and their splendour, for it has been handed over to me, and I give it to anyone I wish. If you, then, worship me, it shall all be yours.' But Jesus answered him, 'It is written:

You shall worship the Lord your God, him alone shall you serve.'

Then he led him to Jerusalem and set him on the parapet of the Temple and said to him, 'If you are Son of God throw yourself down from here, for it is written:

He has given his angels orders about you, to guard you, and that, *They will carry you in their arms in case you trip on a stone.'*

But Jesus answered him, 'It is said:

Do not put the Lord your God to the test.'

Having finished every way of putting him to the test, the devil left him, until the opportune moment.

- If Jesus *had* turned the stone into bread, would it have been a miracle, or merely magic?
- What is the deal Jesus won't strike with Satan?
- What are today's most severe temptations?
- Why do you believe Luke felt he must tell us this story?

ↄ

THIRD BIBLE READING
Mark 10:17–22

He was setting out on a journey when a man ran up, knelt before him and put this question to him, 'Good teacher, what must I do to inherit eternal life?' Jesus said to him, 'Why do you call me good? No one is good but God alone. You know the commandments: You shall not murder; You shall not commit adultery; You shall not steal; You shall not give false witness; You shall not defraud; Honour your father and mother.' And he said to him, 'Teacher, I have kept all these since my youth.' Jesus looked hard at him and loved him and said, 'You are lacking in one thing: go, sell whatever you own and give the money to the poor, and you will have treasure in heaven; then come, follow me.' But at this saying he baulked and he went away grieving, for he had many possessions.

- Why does Mark make a point of saying Jesus loved this young man?
- Can one expand on Bible commandments, as Jesus did?
- Is it faith-less to own many possessions?
- Why do you believe Mark felt he must tell us this story?

A Time for Further Discussion

Meditation – As we prepare for Easter:
Can *you* trust God with all personal, family, community and world problems?

PRAYER
Lord,
We have often prayed for solutions.
We have seldom prayed for salvation.
We have believed we deserve what you bestow
and have asked for more when we have what others
     need.
But we did not truly earn our lives, our loves,
our homes, our bread, our possessions.
We did not earn the world which supports us
or your loving hands which try to turn the world
     to new truth every morning.
As you say, we do not know what we are doing.
We seldom see who we are hurting.
We think of cash and comfort
and yet you love us and forgive us.
Catch us! Hold us! Bear us up
to be richer in spirit.
Amen

PRAYER

Lord,

We have often prayed for solutions.

We have seldom prayed for salvation.

We have believed we deserve what you bestow

and have asked for more when we have what others
need.

But we did not truly earn our lives, our loves,

our homes, our bread, our possessions.

We did not earn the world which supports us

or your loving hands which try to turn the world
to new truth every morning.

As you say, we do not know what we are doing.

We seldom see who we are hurting.

We think of cash and comfort

and yet you love us and forgive us.

Catch us! Hold us! Bear us up

to be richer in spirit.

Amen

SESSION 4

Lost people, being found:
Fogs and the wilderness

PRAYER

FILM CLIPS
Clip 1: 1.21.50 – 1.25.45 London fog
Clip 2: 1.32.35 – 1.34.00 Michael's fog

FOR YOU TO THINK ABOUT

> *'And when the fog comes rolling in,*
> *just keep your feet upon the path'*

In Session 1 we looked at loss. Now we're going to look at *being* lost. To *be lost* is a huge idea, often used in the Bible and still enduring today as a way of expressing a period of emotional disorientation, or of faithlessness. A person who is suffering some kind of emotional crisis or catastrophe can be said to have 'lost their way'. Someone who is judged to have made bad decisions is said to have 'lost the plot'. And to describe someone merely as 'lost', is to suggest that their certainties are gone.

In the past, to 'be lost' had moral overtones. A

woman (yes, nearly always a woman!), who behaved
with sexual impropriety was 'lost' to her family: the
shame she brought them meant that she became 'lost to'
them or 'dead to' them. A 'lost soul' was someone with
no moral compass, or with no sense of the possibility
of salvation. And yet 'lost soul' has the saddest ring to
it ... Jesus would say that no one is lost to God, except
through pride. Pride, in the sense of total self-reliance, is
our voluntary stand against God.

We can be certain that Michael Banks, lost soul
that he is, does not deserve the death of his wife. Nor
does she, come to that! But we could make a case
that Michael's house is being re-possessed owing to
his own fecklessness. So, do we blame him for his
lostness? Certainly, some of the prophets of Hebrew
Scripture would have done so; a strict reading of events
might blame him for (literally) idol-ising Kate. He has
relied on her more entirely than it is safe to rely on
any mortal being. In this day and age, we may find
it difficult to blame someone for loving 'too much' –
but to replace God with a human beloved, is certainly
dangerous.

As Michael becomes more lost, his children's future
looks increasingly bleak. Where will they live? How will
they live? For although we look to Mary Poppins to save
the day, she cannot. She brings along adventures and
excitement, and some fragments of positive philosophy
but she is, ultimately, neither solver nor saviour.

You could argue the Bible is *about* being lost and
being found. Certainly, the theme of lostness, and
of lost causes runs through our scriptures like veins
through granite. From the moment Adam and Eve are
thrown out of the Garden, we have had to confront our
lost-ness.

Think for a moment about one of the huge, glorious story-arcs that the Bible gives us …

Begin with the terrible, unfair lost-ness of the slave Hagar and her son Ishmael, cast out into in the desert. Then think of the rise of the Egyptians (Ishmael's descendants), and their enslavement of the Children of Israel. Then think of the trials and triumphs of Joseph, lost to his over-partial father and his envious brothers, and the sensational reversals of fortune which bring about the family's eventual re-uniting. Then think of Moses, lost to his own enslaved people in his sister's bid to save his life; eventually delivering that people into another kind of forty-year lost-ness in the wilderness.

That *huge* story crosses eons of time, spans vast acreage of land, and covers numerous personal stories of success and failure. It is all about people (and *a* People), constantly being lost and found. And what is this 'lost-ness'? The Bible tells us it is a separation, through attitude or predicament, from our ever-loving God. Doubt and lost-ness are close companions; for when certainty is gone and beliefs falter we are in the wilderness …

The wilderness of the Bible is a place of contradictory dualities. It is a lawless place where commandments are received. It is a place of starvation where manna can be found. It is a place of temptation and of resolve. It is a place of no paths, and of new ways. It is an empty place full of meaning. Mark reports that before Jesus begins his work among us, He enters this empty place of meaning, into 40 days of lost-ness. He intentionally puts himself at the mercy of His hunger, His weakness and His demons. If we believe in these vast and repeating symbols of the Bible, we must take 'as gospel' this notion that hard times are proving times: that to be confronted painfully by our yearnings, deprivations, isolations and temptations is to approach God more closely. Life seems full of trials: those that life supplies – and those we recruit to ourselves.

Bible narrators vary in their understanding of testing times. We are told that Noah and his family are exclusively saved from drowning because Noah is the only good man left in the world. But do *you* believe that floods are God's punishment of faithlessness? Similarly, the Exiles are attributed to a falling-off of faith amongst the tribes of Israel. But do *you* believe that invasions are the fault of those who are invaded? The idea of invasion-as-retribution smacks of the more punishing aspects of 'Prosperity Theology'.

Come to that, where do we stand on the arrival of the Israelites into Canaan and the displacement of the Canaanites? Was invasion by Israelites the upshot of heathen Canaanite faithlessness, or was it simply another rather brutal example of the rain 'falling on the just and the unjust?' (Matthew 4:45).

On their way back from a very disastrous visit to the bank, the children are caught in a thick London fog. The fog is exactly like the predicament they are in: it seems impossible to dispel, overwhelmingly dark – and it is not their fault. They cannot find their way through, but they have Jack the lamp-lighter to shepherd them. They would certainly be lost without him.

Jack holds a semi-evident philosophy about faith and purpose. In the quote at the start of this section he is suggesting that we can choose to stay on a 'path', rather than merely finding a route. Disney has no church in any of its theme-parks and no chapel on board its cruise ships. They steer clear of representing God and avoid religious symbols. So a 'path' is something Disney has traditionally usually fought shy of defining....

There is one significant exception. Satan appears in *Fantasia's* horrifying *Night on Bald Mountain* glorifying in the damnation of lost souls. As an antidote, God's presence is strongly implied in the following *Ave Maria* end-sequence. *Fantasia* the extended film, which was made in 1940, includes much else. But these two sequences are highly unusual for they are not about Disney's usual half-fears and jolly-optimisms; they confront a mortal terror of hell, and lean on overtly religious hope. The two sequences, which belong together, are probably a response to global events of the time. You can view both sequences on YouTube.

Disney have never repeated this experiment, for they are selling happy endings. To invite symbols with too much Meaning is to invite too many questions about God, religion and suffering. They cannot go too far into real life without Meaning getting in the way. However, even Disney lose control of their narrative from time to time, as we saw in Session 3. Disney's attempt to keep faith-themes at bay means that the films must revolve merely around optimism, magic and dreams. In contrast, the Bible *only* deals in real life and in Meaning – even in such stories as Jonah and Job, written as rabbinic pieces to explain the nature of God and faith.

The gravity of the themes of *Mary Poppins Returns* must recruit Jack's 'faith' and 'path' to offer us hope. But Meaning is ultimately castrated. Over time we have barely noticed Disney rendering great themes into small ones for our children. In this 'Fog' section we see lost children, brought home by a keeper of flame. It is a wilderness-and-salvation theme which Disney has introduced but does not dare pursue. Thank God that *we* may.

- Is *feeling* lost the same as *being* lost?
- As a Christian, are you responsible for lost souls?
- What does it mean to 'be found'?

∾

FIRST BIBLE READING
Psalm 107:1-9

'O give thanks to the LORD for he is good;
for his mercy endures for ever.'
Let the redeemed of the LORD say this,
those he redeemed from the hand of the foe
and gathered from far-off lands;
from east and west, north and south.

'They wandered in a barren desert,
finding no way to a city to dwell in.
They were hungry and thirsty;
their soul was fainting within them.

'Then they cried to the LORD in their need,
and he rescued them from their distress,
and he guided them along a straight path,
to reach a city they could dwell in.

'Let them thank the LORD for his mercy,
his wonders for the children of Adam;
for he satisfies the thirsty soul,
and the hungry he fills with good things.'

- What is this Psalm asking of us?
- 'Their souls fainted within them.' What does that mean to you?
- Why do you think there are so many 'wilderness' stories in the Bible?
- Why do you believe the psalmist felt he must tell us this?

೮೨

SECOND BIBLE READING
Luke 15:8-10

'Or again, what woman with ten silver coins would not, if she lost one, light a lamp and sweep out the house and search thoroughly till she found it? And then, when she had found it, call together her friends and neighbours, saying to them, 'Rejoice with me, I have found the silver coin I lost.' In the same way, I tell you, there is rejoicing in the presence of the angels of God over one repentant sinner.'

- How do you feel about Jesus representing God as a woman?
- How does God 'sweep the house and search' for us?
- The precious coin is entirely blameless for its 'lostness'. Must one earn salvation?
- Why do you believe Luke felt he must tell us this story?

೮೨

THIRD BIBLE READING
Mark 14:32-42

They came to a plot of land called Gethsemane, and he said to his disciples, 'Sit here while I pray.' Then he took Peter and James and John with him. And he began to feel dismay and anguish. And he said to them, 'My soul is deeply sorrowful to the point of death. Wait here, and stay awake.' And going on a little further he began falling to the ground and prayed that, if it were possible, this hour might pass away from him. And he said, '*Abba*, Father! For you everything is possible. Take this cup away from me. Yet not what I want but what you want.' He came and found them sleeping, and he said to Peter, 'Simon, are you asleep? Had you not the strength to stay awake one hour? Stay awake and pray not to enter into temptation. The spirit is eager, but flesh is weak.' Again he went away and prayed, saying the same words. And once more he came and found them sleeping, for their eyes were weighed down; and they did not know how they should answer him. He came a third time and said to them, 'Sleep on and have your rest. Enough! The hour has come. See, the Son of man is being betrayed into the hands of sinners. Get up! Let us go! See, my betrayer is not far away.'

- How do you explain Jesus instructing the disciples both to 'Sleep on' and to 'Get up'?
- God does not answer Jesus. Why not?

- Does God take away trouble?
- Why do you believe Mark felt he must tell us this story?

A Time for Further Discussion

Meditation - as we prepare for Easter
As Christians we are taught to pray 'Deliver us from evil'. Some Bible authors tell us that God intervenes. Mark suggests not. Yet still we pray for help ...

PRAYER
Lord of the Lost,
we call to you now,
out of our fogs of pride,
of delight in ourselves,
of despair in each other,
of great clouds of unknowing
to find us, lift us,
to bring us home to you.

Lord of the Found,
we call to you now:
show us how to find our way
from the wilderness to you
next time we wander.
Show us which signs
point us away from you
and those which point us home.
Lord of Celebration,
seeing us far off,
and watching us return,
rejoice yet one more time!
Amen

PRAYER

Lord of the Lost,
we call to you now,
out of our fogs of pride,
of delight in ourselves,
of despair in each other,
our clouds of unknowing
to find us, lift us,
to bring us home to you.

Lord of the Found,
we call to you now:
show us how to find our way
from the wilderness to you
next time we wander.
Show us which signs
point us away from you,
and those which point us home.

Lord of Celebration,
seeing us far off,
and watching us return,
rejoice yet one more time!
Amen

SESSION 5

Light! A seriously heavy symbol ...

PRAYER

FILM CLIPS
Clip 1:   00.31 – 4.20 The philosophy ...
Clip 2:   1.59.06 – 1.59.30 The 'moral'?

FOR YOU TO THINK ABOUT

*'For your light comes with a lifetime
guarantee ...'*

We have mentioned already that this film uses symbols
of great weight, while trying not to get too heavy! But
Light is a symbol that you can't keep 'light'! Light is
the global symbol of new life and new beginnings, of
wisdom and insight and hope. It signifies good over
evil, victory over darkness, knowledge over ignorance.
It expresses our fear of the dark.

In many countries and in many faiths, flames are
a huge part of faith celebrations. Think of the eight
candles of Chanukah, the Advent candles of Christmas,
the flames of Pentecost, the candles of Diwali, the
lantern festivals of Japan and China. Some towns and
villages around the world have their own small, local

festivals of light. If one could accurately complete it, the list would be very, very long.

So we cannot ignore the fact that the *very* first event of *Mary Poppins Returns* is the extinguishing of a flame. Disney is not ignorant of what it means to put out a light: we are being warned of trouble ahead. Jack the Lamplighter is working his patch of London, extinguishing lights under the 'lovely', grey London sky, setting up the idea of a forthcoming darkness. His song reassures us – but the symbol is a grave one; and suitable for us, as we near Good Friday. The Light of the World will, for three horrible days, be extinguished.

Before we can arrive at Easter we must watch the Light of the World put out. We must see God die.

This is never easy. In every generation we have to learn to face Christ's Crucifixion. It is an appalling event to contemplate. In every gathering, there will be people present who want to move briskly over the harrowing story of Christ's betrayal and trial and flogging and denial and torture and death: to skip straight to Easter morning. The horror seems too awful.

And it is. But it doesn't work to skip over it. St Paul stressed that we must 'proclaim Christ crucified'. The resurrection of Christ cannot happen without the Crucifixion of Jesus. The two belong together indivisibly …

It is impossible to imagine how frightened (on so many levels), the disciples felt as they watched things fall apart in the dark days of Jesus' arrest. Even before the Last Supper there will have been a growing feeling of dread at the looming, testing crisis which Jesus had begun to invite and describe. Gospel narratives from Palm Sunday onwards offer us a sense of the mounting danger into which Jesus moves, as he approaches Jerusalem. Good Friday, if we can bear it, invites in the timeless terror and the outrage we feel when we hear about any fixed trial, any false witness, any victory of Evil over Good. These are horrifying in every generation. But then this is not a story with a Disney ending. It is an unending story of complexity and mystery.

Our film has a dark beginning. We have an innocent victim in Michael; his is the crucifixion. We have a truly evil, money-loving villain in William Wilkins. We have little children lost in an actual and emotional fog. But having set up something so dramatic, Disney cannot really 'keep it light'. Hope, knowledge, wisdom, victory, insight, new life: these all have a spiritual and salvational dimensions which Disney, being Disney, leaves mainly unaddressed. Such a symbol of dying light makes us ache for salvation. But there is only one solution here, a financial solution. The film's messiah is ultimately money.

Our question has to be: can we link Lent to anything as relatively lightweight as *Mary Poppins Returns?* I think we can – owing to one character. That character is Jack. It would be easy to see Jack merely as a replacement for Bert, the chimneysweep of the original *Mary Poppins*. But if anyone is representing God in this film, it is Jack. I do not suggest that Disney wishes to present Jack as a godly figure, or as a god; nothing intentional of the sort. (Although we have already seen that this story does not always end up where Disney intends.) I mean that the best parts of humanity – those things within us that are made in God's likeness – are most present in Jack.

Jack is the person who begins the film. He is the only character to speak 'to camera'; in other words, directly to *us*. He is our encourager. It is Jack who tells us what to hope, what to expect, how to trust. While other characters are each caught up only in their own story, Jack has an overarching perspective. His is the widest view: he recognises the crisis in the city and the trouble in the Banks family. He knows that storms are brewing, he believes in joyful resolution. Seen through a classical eye, he seems like a prophet! He may be heralding doom and gloom. But unlike many prophets, biblical or present-day, there is a very soft side to Jack. He is the person who brings the lost children home.

Jack also belongs, thoroughly, to the wider world beyond Cherry Tree Lane. He is tied up with other people, not with himself. He is part of the joyful host of men who bring light to the city. In their perilous attempt to put back the clock, he is the bravest. Mary Poppins eventually weighs in with her magic umbrella, but it is Jack, with human determination and mortal sinew who risks the ascent of the many wavering ladders up to the clock face. To the extent that Jack has no perceivable need, except to serve others, he is Christ-like.

From the outset we imagined that Mary Poppins would resolve, with demure heroics, the difficulties of the plot. We were mistaken. She has been fun and mysterious and magical but she is too self-involved to be truly empathic and too unassailable to require courage. Neither Mary nor Jack resolve the problems of the story. But Jack turns out to be the unassuming and sympathetic hero. If there is anything miraculous in this film, it is Jack's human endeavour.

Jesus rejected magic. In the wilderness he turned away from instant food, conjuring tricks, and power without responsibility. In spite of all his miracles, there is nothing magical about Jesus. And Jack, too, is down to earth. Magic does not contain love. Miracles implicitly do. Magic can be dark. Miracles are not.

Surprisingly – and unintentionally – this film offers us a chance to contrast Mary's magical, effortless solutions against the loving risks taken by a bringer of light. Can you imagine that!

- See how many Bible references to light you can remember
- Why are we frightened of darkness?
- Does this film cast any light?

ల

FIRST BIBLE READING
1 Samuel 3:1-3

Now, the boy Samuel was serving the LORD in the presence of Eli. In those days it was rare for the LORD to speak; visions were uncommon. One day, it happened that Eli was lying down in his room. His eyes were beginning to grow dim; he could no longer see.

The lamp of God had not yet gone out …

- Light is not mentioned here. So why is it central?
- What is the connection between 'visions' and Eli's eyesight?
- What is the Lamp of God?
- Why do you believe this writer felt he must tell us this story?

ↄ

SECOND BIBLE READING
Matthew 17:1-5

Six days later, Jesus took with him Peter and James and his brother John and led them up a high mountain on their own. In their presence he was transfigured: his face shone like the sun and his clothes became as dazzling as light. And suddenly Moses and Elijah appeared to them, talking with him. Then Peter spoke to Jesus, saying, 'Lord, it is wonderful for us to be here; if you want me to, I will make three shelters here, one for you, one for Moses and one for Elijah.' He was still speaking when suddenly a bright cloud covered them with shadow, and suddenly from the cloud there came a voice which said, 'This is my Son, the Beloved; he enjoys my favour. Listen to him.'

- What is the significance of this story?
- How could one be overshadowed by a bright cloud?
- What is silly about Peter's suggestion?
- Why do you believe Matthew felt he must tell us this story?

ↄ

THIRD BIBLE READING
Mark 15:33-34

When noon came there was darkness over the whole land until mid-afternoon. And at that time Jesus cried out in a loud voice, '*Eloi, eloi, lama sabachthani?*' which means, '*My God, my God, why have you forsaken me?*'

- What do you think is meant by the whole land?
- What does this particular darkness signify?
- How might you connect this story to our other two readings?
- Why do you believe Mark felt he must tell us this?

A Time for Further Discussion

Meditation – as we prepare for Easter
The Light of the World dies from betrayal and torture; and unlike those first disciples, approaching the Good Friday murder, *we* know what happens on the third day. But let us stay with the darkness to imagine what they went through – and thank God that we don't have to…

PRAYER
Great God, the world is dark sometimes,
and mostly that belongs with us,
in all those things we didn't do:
to stay awake, to honour you
to clothe you, feed you, stay with you,

to watch and pray, and visit you.
We know well what we do.

Great God, the world is dark sometimes,
and mostly that belongs with us,
who have avoided your command,
who have not loved or lent a hand
to those in prison, on the street,
cold, and with not enough to eat.
We know well what we do.

Cast light on what we haven't done
so that we see what we must do.
Cast light on petty games we play
to stop ourselves from helping you.
Cast light on all our daily tricks
which separate our souls from you.
We know well what we do.

Cast light on envies, enmities,
all the untruths which promise much.
Cast light on purses firmly closed
and over wallets never touched.
Cast light so true we cannot lie,
which will not let us pass on by.
We know well what we do.

Great God, the world is dark sometimes
and mostly that belongs with us.
You are among us, everywhere
Rough-sleeping on the high-road there
without the food we would not share.
Light up the fact we did not care!
We know well what we do.

LEADERS'
PAGES

LEADERS:
AN APPRECIATION
AND A PLAN

'Practically Perfect in Every Way!'

Group leaders need some appreciation. They're pretty selfless. Courses would certainly be a muddle without them. We thank you for taking responsibility for creating a paced and thoughtful session.

You are the ones charged with:

- Turning potential disputes back into discussions
- Containing the group through sad or hard feelings
- Noticing who's being left out
- Allowing silences
- Reminding people of the question!
- Knowing how to move discussion on
- Discerning when discussion is too fruitful to hurry.

If your talents cover some (but not all) of the above, then recruit help. You may feel comfortable managing everything; but it might be more easy – and more enjoyable – to split the load.

Every group has its own little ways! If your group

includes one or two 'new' people, or is made up of other smaller groups, people may not share as freely. If it's a small and intimate group, it may be more difficult to move a 'stuck record' discussion on. If your group is very big, it might need splitting into smaller groups for discussion.

If you belong within the group you serve, you will already know the particular challenges you face. Resistance to change? Mistrust of strangers? Alarm at new ideas? Over-assertive ways of stating faith? Inflexible biblical interpretation? Or just very strong characters?! Draw comfort from this: Jesus faced all these things. You're not alone.

Not all questions in this book are conventional, and there are some broader questions raised on pp. 99-100? which you may consider helpful to introduce. The group may be tempted to skate round perfectly pertinent questions. But don't *you* be tempted. Help them dig down …

You will find a section on the songs of the film, which some people may find helpful and there are Bible references for those who enjoy deeper study. Some groups love long sessions, others *really* don't. It's your group and your time-limit, so we have left the timings to you. (For example, if your weekly session is short, it may be necessary to choose *two* Bible readings, rather than three).

Below is a skeleton session-plan which works for any length of session. You don't have to follow it, but it offers a solid structure.

Session Plan – this applies to all sessions

1. Group members arrive having (hopefully!) read the relevant Session Chapter.
2. Warn the group:

'We will start in exactly FIVE MINUTES! If you are not sitting down by then, I'm starting anyway.'

3. Short opening prayer – from a group member or from yourself.
4. Remind the group about confidentiality
5. Group watches film clips
6. Group discusses session chapter and chapter questions
7. First Bible reading and discussion of the attached questions
8. Break – length to be decided by you, in advance
9. Warn the group again (!)
   'We will start in exactly TWO MINUTES!
   If you are not sitting down by then, I'm starting anyway.'
10. Second (and/or third?) Bible reading and discussion of attached questions
11. Wider questions from the group or from the *Other Questions* section
12. Meditation and Closing Prayer

Your leaders' notes, for each session are at the back of the book. They are short and to the point. If you wish to look up song lyrics in full, they are at lyricfind.com

Performed songs are all available to hear (though mostly *not* to view) on YouTube.

Phew! Well done, good and faithful servant ...

SESSION 1:
LEADERS' NOTES

Film clips: '*When you wish upon a star…*'
Clip 1: 00.00 – 00.30 The *Disney* ident
Clip 2: 23.00 – 26.00 Mary's return to 17 Cherry Tree
Lane
Clip 3: 1.55.16 – 1.57.50 Michael remembers

The theme and the group
This session is all about beliefs and believing. All the way through this course your group will be talking about their beliefs. This first session is your chance to set the tone for how people listen to each other.

However obvious it may seem, it's important for you to point out to the group that they are a collection of *very* different people with different ways of believing; and that their varied ideas will enrich the discourse. Our beliefs are part of who we are; but they may also change, as we ourselves do. Beliefs may be questioned, but not attacked. Exploring our beliefs and our doubts is part of our preparation for Easter. Jesus is with us as we do it.

No judging!
In discussions like these, no-one should be judged for what they do – or don't – believe. Almost everyone's

faith and beliefs are developing and fluid, not fixed. To 'know' about God (except in terms of one's own singular relationship with God) goes contrary to 'having faith'. As Paul says, 'we know only in part and we can prophesy only in part'.

A helpful reminder for a tentative group is Mark 9:24: 'At once the father of the boy cried out, "I have faith. Help my lack of faith!"'

SESSION 2:
LEADERS' NOTES

Film clips: *Can we reconcile these two songs?*
Clip 1:   15.48 – 18.18 'A Conversation'
Clip 2:   58.20 – 1.02.28 'The Place Where Lost
           Things Go'

This is a session about change and loss. Change is the only entirely predictable thing in life .... but we don't like it and we didn't like it in Jesus' time either!

Everyone in your group will be undergoing change of some kind, even if they don't want to think about it. Some people may be having to plan how they will cope with getting older. Some will be changing work, or moving homes, or watching children leave the nest. Some will be expecting a new baby – or grand-baby. Some will be grieving a loved one, or a broken relationship. Some may be worried about developments in church, community or family. Some may be alarmed at the turn of recent politics. Some will be sad, and some may express anger. There is a time for all these things. Sadness and anger (and hilarity of course!) all belong in the group to be expressed. But not temper.

If your group is smallish and intimate, it may be possible to discuss loss openly. If it is not, it may be worth asking people to pair up for the first half of the discussion, before coming back to talk in the main group. This will allow for confidences to be shared and feelings to be expressed which might not otherwise reach the group at all.

The most comforting of the three Bible readings for this session is probably Ecclesiastes. It would be wise, if time is short, to keep this reading and forfeit one of the others. As always, make sure that the people with quiet or timid voices are able to speak.

Whether we like it or not, Jesus can be the imperative for change which we resist the most – and thus the greatest challenge.

SESSION 3: LEADERS' NOTES

Film clips: *Is this a children's story?*
Clip 1:   53.15 – 57.45 Georgie's nightmare.
Clip 2:   1.48.40 – 1.50.28 The real nightmare

This session is about money versus idolatry. The group will be asking itself about trust in money and trust in God. This a never-ending issue, not solely for the consideration of individuals. It will be worth reminding the group of this. Businesses must work out what to keep in reserve and what to risk. Charities, hospitals, prisons, governments, schools must balance what they spend on employees against what resources are provided for end-users. Faith institutions must monitor whether their funds are disposed to self-serve or to serve… All these aspects of trust are worth bringing up.

The questions for this session are quite challenging; it is easy to concentrate on controlling not trusting. As leader, it is worth remembering that there will be people in your group from different economic backgrounds. You may need to make sure that the wealthier people do not hold the floor: it will be 'richer' to hear a contrast of ways of living. As you all consider your faith in the light of the film, it may be worth pointing the group to Timothy 6:10, This is often misquoted. Money is not the root of all evil. The precise quotation is: 'The root of all evils is the love of money'.

SESSION 4:
LEADERS' NOTES

Film clips: *Two kinds of lost-ness*
Clip 1:   1.21.50 – 1.25.45 London fog
Clip 2:   1.32.35 – 1.34.00 Michael's fog

Being lost is a frightening subject. Many of us remember a moment, as children, when we became separated from our parents. People from some cultural backgrounds (Rwanda and Kosovo being only two examples) never saw their parents again. Think ahead to the sensibilities of refugees and asylum seekers in your group and do your best to prevent less subtle group-members attempting to gloss over, or minimise, their pain. Crucifixions are all around us in different forms; if we do not allow their expression in Lent, then we are not *having* Lent! The fact of Jesus' Crucifixion and Resurrection is not, for everyone, an escape from pain, but an affirmation of surviving it.

If you know that there are delicate issues and/or vulnerable people in the group, it may be better that the provided questions are discussed in pairs. Being lost is rich material for a discussion of great depth; the wildernesses which some people have endured – and still endure – lend perspective to our own. Ask the group (but not any one individual) what temptations they found in the wilderness. It will link you back, helpfully, to considering how Jesus dealt with his own temptations.

Being lost will mean different things to different people. Some may talk of dementia, or mental illness, or bereavement, or divorce, or the loss of a child, or crippling loneliness, or addiction, or infirmity. Again, it will be your job (with, if necessary, a kind and robust helper), to gently close down competitive suggestions that one kind of lost-ness is worse than another (!).

If anyone seems still to be in their wilderness by the end of the session, please, stay with them for a while *and* phone them later. If you do not feel up to this, have someone standing by who will. The approach to Easter is about truth and suffering. We are not here to avoid that, but to minister to it.

SESSION 5: LEADERS' NOTES

Film clips*: Only a little gravity*
Clip 1:   00.31 – 4.20 The philosophy …
Clip 2:   1.59.06 – 1.59.30 The 'moral?

This session is about light and darkness, and implicitly about hope. As Christians we hold to the truth that 'light shines in darkness, and darkness could not overpower it' (John 1:5). But we have dark Good Friday immediately before us, and there is no Easter without that. So it will be important that the group speaks about what Good Friday means.

There is horror of more than one kind in the Good Friday story. Firstly, there is the narrative itself which describes powerful people brutally abusing their power. Secondly, there is the shocking loneliness of Jesus, with friends asleep and running away; followed by the all-too-human denials of Peter. Thirdly, there is the question of whether Jesus was 'destined' by his Father to die – or whether he chose a ministry which would end up in his death.

This third strand can be very uncomfortable. Perhaps group members may wish to discuss to what extent they believe Jesus *had* agency. Such discussions are all to the good: the group will be doing deep theology. But make sure that all opinions receive polite attention and do not permit people with rigid orthodoxies to scold.

Good Friday is the grim door to hope. People have told me very dark stories of 'Good Friday' moments which end in unexpected resurrections. When we are in times of trial, of despair, of pain, we cannot recognise them as possible portals to joy. We believe that we are in the grip of something eternally deathly. There may be people who wish to explore the 'dark-before-the-dawn' aspects of their own experience.

Dear Patient Leader, in the face of severe temptation, thank you for keeping your humour, your temper and your nerve for the last forty days and forty nights…

OTHER QUESTIONS

The narrative of *Mary Poppins Returns* raises questions which we might not expect. Here are a few questions about that.

- What makes a film good or bad?
- Must films be believable?
- Must Bible stories be believable?
- What is this film about?
- Is the world of the film anything like your world?
- Who is the film for?
- Is the lack of diversity justified?
- Is there evil in this film?
- Where is God in the film?
- Why is Jane in the film?
- What is the role of the 'Leeries' in this film?
- Why do some people describe Easter as 'a Disney story'?
- What is the film saying about:

    - Death?
    - Money?
    - Poverty?

- What is true about this film?
- Has the film a clear message?
- What is Mary's function in this film?

- Is there retribution in the story?
- Why is this film not set in the present day?
- Why not have a black Mary Poppins?

THE SONGS:
A FUNNY MIXTURE

There is a lot of fun running through this film, along with some nonsense and some serious themes. In fact, the songs differ a great deal in substance. Looking at them one by one may help you to hear individual points of interest or enjoyment. Looking at them overall they present a puzzle. Anyway, here goes!

1. **(Underneath the) Lovely London Sky**
   This opening song is sung by Jack the Lamplighter, extinguishing lights on a dim London morning. His song functions to introduce us to London, to the Banks Household, and in broader terms, to the predicaments of both. Jack is being fondly ironic about the sky of his home town, because it remains, throughout the song, the dull and unlovely grey so familiar to Londoners past and present.

   He sings about borrowed money, broken crockery and the 'Slump'. But both his song and his way of singing are energetic and positive; we are told to count our blessings, count ourselves lucky, and hold onto those we love because 'maybe soon, from up above, you'll be blessed': This idea of a blessing, in the script a secular film, seems to be guaranteeing us a happy ending, if we have faith.

The older viewers among us will remember Mary Poppins departing into the London sky in the original film. She returns on the string of a kite (as she does in P. L. Travers second book, *Mary Poppins Comes Back*). Has she been lurking, immaculately, behind a cloud for all those decades? Probably.

2. A Conversation

Michael's almost-spoken song gives us a touching glimpse of an isolated soul mourning his wife, Kate. Sung alone, with little breath and much pathos, the song shows us Michael's grief. He can hear his late wife's voice in his silences. He misses her wisdom, her advice, her conversation, her guidance in bringing up their children. The pace, meter and rhyme of this song are all entirely regular – and symbolic of Kate's predictable regularity which Michael is missing. He is expressing a life turned barren. It is a lonely little song and without hope. The placing of Jack's song, prior to this, ensures that we remain optimistic. But Kate will not be coming back. Mary will.

This is a glimpse of a private moment. It might also be a secret moment. It is interesting to contrast Michael's unfunny, sweet song about his personal feelings with the comic depiction of his father's difficulties in the previous film. Perhaps Western audiences, and this Disney, are less judgmental about evident male suffering than they might have been in the 1960s.

3. Can You Imagine That?

This is the rollicking bath-time song, mostly sung underwater, which introduces the three young Banks children to the astonishing side of Mary Poppins. It is about imagination and optimism versus logic. It begins by suggesting that 'intellect can wash away confusion' and ends up stating that 'some stuff and nonsense could be fun'.

This tension between the sensible and the dreamlike is at the heart of all *Mary Poppins* books and the earlier film. Mary pretends at all times to be solid, rational, conventional, while actually being magical and unpredictable. Perhaps P. L. Travers' ideal environment for a growing child is precisely this mix of the utterly stable and the fantastic.

There is an intriguing little line which may refer to Mary herself, but which also sounds like a reference to the lost Boys of J. M. Barrie's *Peter Pan*. It is: *'They won't grow up and don't grow old'*. We never quite know, in this song, whether Mary is admitting to a liking for fun. She will, of course, deny it later.

4. The Royal Doulton Music Hall

A lovely romp, very nicely written, about a place where animals meet for entertainment. Similar to Burlesque, though less raunchy, British 'Music Hall' entertainment started in early Victorian times and was a kind of variety show made up mostly of songs and stand-up comedy with appearances from the occasional ventriloquist act, or dance troupe. If you look on the internet you can see ancient film-clips of some of the most famous 'turns', the 'Egyptian Sand Dance' being one that toured for many decades. Some music-hall songs were sentimental, some comic, and some thoroughly and unashamedly improper: the great Marie Lloyd sang a hugely popular number which began, 'She sits among the cabbages – and peas', which she was forced, by law, to change for decency's sake. By that evening the line had changed to 'She sits among the cabbages - and leeks'.

There were music-hall theatres in all major British cities and they tended not to be situated in wealthy areas. Music-hall artists became very famous and would continually move round Britain performing their acts. Audiences could be rowdy and heckling was frequent, although an audience might be won round by performers who put a heckler down in a particularly witty way. Later theatres provided food and drink in the auditorium, leading to food being thrown at unpopular acts. Mary and Jack are singing this song with a proper music-hall delivery, but get properly into their 'act' in the next song.

5. A Cover is Not the Book

This piece is nearer to Burlesque. It is sung fast and performed hard. The central idea is that people are not always what they seem, and that we shouldn't judge people too quickly. We make mistakes about people and they make mistakes about us. But the song has missed the most dangerous aspect of our rash judgements: the huge errors we can routinely about people of other faiths, tribes, classes, cultures, colours, genders. The Good Samaritan parable is Jesus' elegant way of pointing out that the cover is *not* the book.

The song is dealing gently with rash judgements. But it is also encouraging us to read more books, while paying homage to story-lines from another

Mary Poppins book. Mary begins by singing about an 'Uncle Gutenberg', who doesn't appear in the Poppins books at all.

His mention is an obscure and veiled reference to the Gutenberg Bible, printed in the 1400s; the first Bible available to the secular, wealthy public; also, to today's Gutenberg Project, 60,000 eBooks, available online, copyright-free to the public. Both 'Gutenbergs' references could be seen as (obscure) encouragements to read …

Both Nellie Rubina ('made of wood') and the Dirty Rascal ('the king may be a crook') are characters from *Mary Poppins Comes Back*, the second P. L. Travers' book. Hyacinth McCaw is the name of a South American jungle bird; an in-joke about Mary's talkative umbrella-handle, modelled on that very same bird.

Disney hopefully intends some lyrics to go over the heads of any children watching; they are suggestive in a way that the original film was not. But we have to ask ourselves whether this song has accessible meaning to anyone, beyond the solid old adage: 'Don't judge a book by its cover.'

6. The Place Where Lost Things Go

We explore the meaning and intention of this song fully in Session 2, but here are a few more thoughts. Mary's intention seems more straightforward than her song. Watching the film-clip may help you decide what is – and what is not – being faced. It is most certainly a song of answers: each verse covers and then relieves an anxiety. Perhaps it is the antidote to *A Conversation*, the bleak song of widowed Michael.

Mary is reassuring Michael's children that their mother is not '*lost without trace*'. The song is a very good example of the optimism with which Disney infuses dark themes. But what does Mary's whimsy actually mean: '*Maybe on the moon, or maybe somewhere new, maybe all you're missing lives inside of you*'? Children need comfort, but don't they also deserve clarity?

7. Turning Turtle

The children have broken a Doulton bowl of their late mother's and they set off to Mary Poppins' cousin Topsy Turvy, to see if she can mend it. When they arrive, her house is literally upside down; not merely untidy, but up-ended. The clever little lyrics open up the idea that it's good to get a different point of view, and to see things from angles other than your own. This upside-down song is a metaphor for the children's recent life.

Perhaps this is the most joyfully performed of all the songs. Topsy is quirky, sparky and amusingly flirtatious with Jack. The writing is flexible and witty, owing partly to the grammatical errors which Topsy's European origins allow. But this is, ostensibly, a children's film, so I wonder about lyrics which are beyond children's comprehension. Most can be followed on a second or third hearing, but the mention of Tolstoy is a puzzle in more ways than one …

8. Trip a Little Light Fantastic

This is a song about losing one's bearings and getting them back; a song about attitude. It develops the optimism of Jack's opening song.

The children are lost in two kinds of fog: a London 'pea-soup' fog and a murky problem. Jack and a crowd of jolly, dancing 'Leeries' (lamplighters) bring them home.

This energising song is doing the same job, in a much bouncier way, as *The Place Where Lost Things Go* each verse sets up a dark problem to extinguish. There is, though, a difference between Mary's and Jack's way of offering help. It is hidden in Jack's refrain. We could guess that the intention behind Mary's song is that the children should absorb her words, think about them, and take comfort from them. That is the extent of her engagement.

But for Jack, each refrain – '*Trip a little light fantastic, with **me**'* – is an invitation to come to him when heavily burdened. It is a relational song which Mary's is not. We know (do we not?) that Mary will disappear one day ... whereas Jack will stay.

Jack suggests that we have agency within our suffering; that our perspective is a choice: '*When you're alone in your room, your choice is: just embrace the gloom. Or, you can trip a little light fantastic with **me**'*. Jack is a hopeful pragmatist.

9. Nowhere to Go But Up!

There are echoes, throughout this second film, of the first *Mary Poppins* film. Both have big 'cockney' dance numbers. Both have fantasy sections incorporating cartoon characters. Both end with songs of restoration and peace. '*Let's go fly a kite*' was the refrain of the first film, with the family and the wider community in the park, enjoying themselves, with the emphasis on the sky, to which Mary must return.

A cheery Balloon Lady is selling both balloons and ideas. She is a far cuter old lady than the Bird Woman who was obviously a figure for sympathy.

It is at this point in the film that Michael, relieved of all his fears, realises that the impossible things he recalled about Mary Poppins are all true. His dark clouds have dispersed, the sky is clear ahead: 'Let the past take a bow, the forever is now.' It is an entirely hopeful song at the end of a challenging journey. It is a cheerful song about happy futures and cheerful endings.